Embroidered MANDALAS

LARK

New York

Embroidered
MANDALAS

25 IRON-ON MANDALA DESIGNS TO STITCH, COLOR, AND SHARE

New York

An Imprint of Sterling Publishing Co., Inc.
1166 Avenue of the Americas
New York, NY 10036

ISBN 978-1-4547-1041-7

Distributed in Canada by Sterling Publishing Co., Inc.
c/o Canadian Manda Group, 664 Annette Street
Toronto, Ontario, M6S 2C8, Canada
Distributed in the United Kingdom by GMC Distribution Services
Castle Place, 166 High Street, Lewes, East Sussex, BN7 1XU, England
Distributed in Australia by NewSouth Books
University of New South Wales, Sydney, NSW 2052, Australia

For information about custom editions, special sales, and premium
and corporate purchases, please contact Sterling Special Sales
at 800-805-5489 or specialsales@sterlingpublishing.com.

Manufactured in China

2 4 6 8 10 9 7 5 3

sterlingpublishing.com
larkcrafts.com

Photographs by Chris Bain
All mandala illustrations by iStockphoto.com and/or Shutterstock.com
Cover design by Igor Satanovsky.
Embroidery stitch illustrations: Dorothy Dennis (front), Dansare Marks,
Emily Tirella, Joy Holder Northrop, and Orrin Lundgren (back)

mandalas have been used in various cultures as an aid to meditation. In this book the aim is to create beautiful pieces, to soothe, and to embroider the designs with minimal effort. Each mandala contained here is easily transferable onto cloth and then framed within the hoop you use for embroidery.

EMBROIDERY BASICS

Most materials for embroidery are relatively inexpensive and available at local craft supply stores or online.

MATERIALS AND TOOLS

- 8″ (20.5 cm) diameter embroidery hoop
- Embroidery needles
- Embroidery floss/thread
- Fabric stabilizer
- Fabric pens
- Iron and ironing board or flat surface
- Lead pencil
- Nonpermanent fabric markers
- Pins
- Ruler
- Scissors
- Thimble

Fabrics

Almost any fabric can be used for embroidery, but the best choices are embroidery fabric, quilter's cotton, or large-weave cotton cloth. Embroidery fabric—sold in craft stores and online—comes in different weaves and counts. There is *Aida*, known as a block weave (most popular count is 14); *Hardanger*, also a block weave, with a 22 thread count; and linen, which can be quite expensive. Even-weave fabrics are best for cross stitch. Delicate materials like silk and chiffon require special care so the fabric does not become stretched out or distorted. Heavier materials (denim) are harder to stitch through. Fabric stabilizers should be applied on stretchy fabrics (such as T-shirts) so that they are strong enough to withstand the embroidery stitching without puckering, dimpling, or gapping.

Embroidery Floss/Thread

Embroidery floss comes in a small bundle in an array of colors. Manufacturers number each thread color so that you can pick up the same color whenever you want to. Embroidery floss is made up of six strands twisted together. For some of the more intricate patterns in this book you may want to separate the threads into three strands. For the basic shape, however, six strands are fine.

Needles

A basic embroidery needle is medium-sized with a sharp point and a wider eye than regular sewing needles for ease of threading. Most craft stores and online retailers carry packets of multiple needles in different sizes. Purchasing these will ensure that you have the needle size you need.

Embroidery Hoops

Embroidery hoops come in different sizes, anywhere from 3" (7.5 cm) to 12" (30.5 cm), both in wood and plastic. For these projects you will need an 8" (20.5 cm) hoop, but you may want to pick up a smaller hoop for ease of reach.

DESIGN TRANSFER ESSENTIALS

Iron-On Transfer

The iron-on transfers in this book make moving the design to fabric easy. You'll need an iron and an ironing board or a flat hard surface with cloth. If you're not using cotton or an embroidery fabric, test how well the transferring works. Here's how: Set your iron on the highest heat. Spread your fabric on the ironing board (your fabric should be big enough to center the mandala with additional room to pull it tight on the hoop). Press the hot iron down onto the transfer firmly. Keep the iron still. Lift the iron after several seconds; then move onto another section and repeat. Press the entire transfer for 20–30 seconds. After that time, if it has not worked, press it for a bit longer. The transfers are reusable up to four or five times.

TRADITIONAL TRANSFER METHOD

If you would like to add something to a design in this book, start by copying it onto tracing paper or making a photocopy. Depending on what fabric you are using, you may be able to trace the lines with a lead pencil or a nonpermanent fabric maker.

The ink in fabric markers may be washed out or it may fade away. For longer projects, washable ink is preferable.

Press your fabric before you transfer your design.

Light Method

An easy way to get a design on light-colored fabric is to trace it by using a light source, such as a light box, under your fabric. Tape the design over the lighted area, place the fabric over the design, and trace the design with a pencil or a fabric pen.

Carbon Paper Method

Dressmakers' carbon paper is available at many craft stores. It comes in light and dark colors to contrast with your fabric color. Place your fabric on a hard surface, put the carbon paper on top of it, and then place the design on top of the carbon paper. Tape or pin the design in place so that it does not move when you are tracing it. Using a blunt pen or pencil, trace over the design (press down hard), and the carbon will make the design marks on your fabric. If you are missing some elements of the design, you can fill these in with a fabric pen.

Preparing Fabric

Stretchy, loose-weave fabrics are difficult to embroider unless you apply a stabilizer first. Stabilizers are easy to apply and keep the fabric from stretching out while you are working. This ensures a better finished project.

Sticky-back stabilizers are easy to work with since you can stitch right through them. When you are done with your embroidery, simply carefully tear them away.

Hoop and Thread

Even with the stabilizer, be sure to use a hoop. Spread your fabric over the smaller hoop and fit the larger one over the top. Use the small screw to tighten and pull the edges of the fabric so that it is smooth and taut.

If your fabric has ragged edges, you may want to tape them while you are embroidering.

Thread your needle, and pull the thread through the eye. (If you are having trouble threading the needle, you can dampen the tip of the thread to make it stiffer and push it through.) Knot the bottom of the thread once you have your needle threaded.

STITCHING

You can stitch either by section or by color. If you stitch by color, you can get a sense of how much floss you will use. Pull the thread through the fabric, making sure it is secured by the knot. When you are near the end of your strand, push the needle through the back and then loop it under a stitch a few times. Alternatively, you can finish off by tying the ends together on the back of the project.

Stitch Library

All the stitches listed here are used in the mandalas. If you are new to some stitches, get a practice cloth and experiment. It is easier to do this than to rip out your stitches!

Have fun and relax while you embroider these beautiful designs.

BACKSTITCH

Creates a solid line. Make a small stitch, then bring the needle back up through the fabric (A) and stitch back to meet the initial stitch at (B). Keep all stitches uniform in length and tension so that your line is clean and can be used to outline shapes.

BLANKET STITCH

Often used for finishing off edges. Starting at the design line (A), make a diagonal stitch (loose) away from line (B). Bring the needle up to the front of the fabric on the design line, then slip the needle under and pull tight to the design line or the fabric edge. Make a new diagonal stitch to the right, and repeat, slipping on each stitch as you go (C).

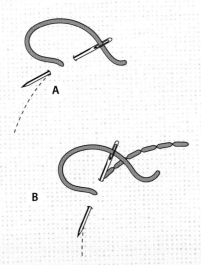

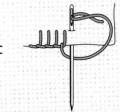

CHAIN STITCH

Has the look of a chain when it's done. Pull the needle through the fabric (A), and poke the needle back into the fabric at (A) to create a loop ⅛"–¼" (3–6 mm) long (B). Pull the needle through the fabric at (B) to secure the loop (C) and repeat, making a new loop and creating a chain. To secure the last loop, make a tiny stitch at the top (D).

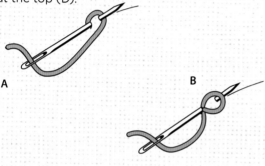

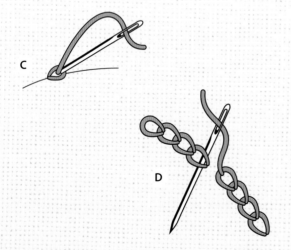

CROSS STITCH

Even stitches that each look like an "X." This stitch is often used to create a different texture and to fill in large spaces. Make a small diagonal (A to B), then make a second stitch across this (C to D). Pull the needle through at (A) and repeat the process to make a line of cross stitches. To create a long line of cross stitch, make a row of diagonal stitches, then stitch across backwards down the line.

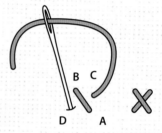

FLY STITCH

Consists of two stitches—a loose long stitch and a short tacking stitch. A fly stitch can be used as a decorative stitch to fill in spaces. Bring the needle through the fabric and make a loose stitch (from A to B). Bring the needle back up through the center of the loop (C), and back down to tack the loop into the shape of a "V (D)."

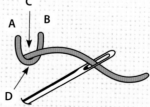

FRENCH KNOT

Creates a three-dimensional knot, used often for eyes, in the center of flowers or for other dotted elements. Bring the needle through the top of the fabric, wrap the thread around the tip of the needle twice, and then place the needle back at the point where you pulled it through. Pull the needle back down through the thread, and pull tight.

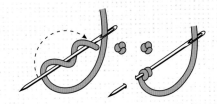

LAZY DAISY

A detached chain stitch that creates a floral pattern. Pull the needle through the fabric at (A), then pull it back in at (A) to make a loose loop. Secure it with a small stitch at (B). Continue to do the chain stitch in a circle to create a flower design.

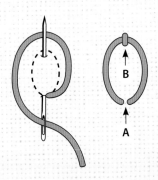

SATIN STITCH

Often used to fill in a space. Make a straight stitch from (A) to (B), a second stitch directly next to it, and so forth. If you have a design line, start and end your straight stitch on the line.

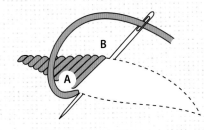

SCALLOP STITCH

Similar in technique to chain stitch but with additional space between stitches. Bring the needle up at (A), make a loose stitch down at (B), and secure with a small stitch in the middle of C and D to make a loop.

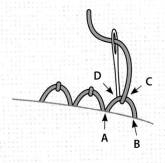

SPLIT STITCH

In this stitch you are literally making a split in the threads. A split stitch works well to create an outline. Make stitch (A to B) that is twice as long as desired. At point (C) push the needle through between the thread to split it in half. Repeat, making another long stitch and then splitting the threads in half.

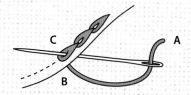

STAR STITCH

Similar to cross stich but with an additional stitch. Make a small diagonal (A to B), then make a second stitch across this (C to D). Add an additional line across (E to F). For the circle method, make several small stitches in a circle to create a star. You can add as many additional lines as you desire.

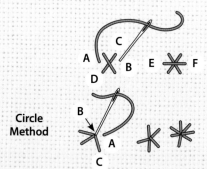

STEM STITCH

Make a stitch (A to B), leaving the thread loose, and pull it back through midway (C). Pull tight. Continue on like this for the length of the design line.

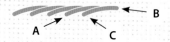

STRAIGHT STITCH

(also known as a running stitch): As indicated, a straight stitch is made along a design line—no looping or crossing involved. A straight stitch is also good for creating outlines. Simply pull the needle and thread through the fabric and back in on a straight line. Leave as big a space as desired between stitches.

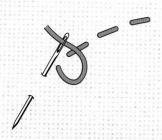